How to Feel More Comfortable on Camera

Gillian Whitney

304 S Jones Blvd Suite 4438

Las Vegas, NV 89107

ISBN: 979-8-8595-1668-1

Paperback edition 20230830.C

Contents

Introduction

"Inaction breeds doubt and fear. Action breeds confidence and courage. If you want to conquer fear, do not sit home and think about it. Go out and get busy."

~ Dale Carnegie

For many people, the thought of being on camera is enough to make them break out in a cold sweat. But it doesn't have to be that way. With a little practice and some simple tips, you can learn to feel more comfortable on camera and use it to your advantage. Whether you want to get started with live streaming or make recorded videos, the more you can feel comfortable on camera, the more confident you'll become.

Being on camera can feel very unnatural and make people uncomfortable. However, with video becoming such an important aspect of our personal and professional communication, it's a skill everyone needs to develop.

In this book, I'll share with you everything I've learned about how to feel more comfortable on camera with regards to both live and recorded video.

I'll cover topics like:

- Having a sense of humor
- Overcoming self-limiting beliefs
- What to wear
- What to talk about
- Importance of storytelling
- Warming up before you begin
- Managing your time
- How Toastmasters can help you
- How to avoid memorizing your lines
- What tech you really need to get started with video

I'll also share with you some of my own personal experiences with being on camera. I'll tell you about the times I've made mistakes, the times I've succeeded, and the lessons I've learned along the way.

I hope this book will help you feel more comfortable on camera and encourage you to use video to share your message with the world.

Who This Book Is For

This book is for anyone who wants to feel more comfortable on camera. Whether you're a business owner, a marketer, a job seeker, or just someone who wants to share your thoughts and ideas with the world, this book will help you get started. The tips and tactics in this book are relevant whether you're interested in live or recorded video.

How to Use This Book

This book is designed to be a quick read. It's a practical guide to feeling more comfortable on camera. You can read it from cover to cover, or you can pick and choose the chapters that are most relevant to you.

I encourage you to read the book with a pen and paper in hand. Take notes and highlight the important points. Just know that the more time you spend in front of the camera, the more comfortable you'll become on camera.

I'm Excited to Help You

I'm excited to help you feel more comfortable on camera. I know that it can be a daunting task, but it's also an incredibly rewarding one. When you're able to share your message with the world, you can make a real difference.

So, let's get started!

Chapter 1

Take the First Step

"Man plans and God Laughs."

~ Yiddish Proverb

Feeling uncomfortable on camera? You're not alone. Many people struggle with this, especially introverts. But it's important to overcome this fear if you want to share your message with the world.

My Video Journey

I'm an introvert myself, and I used to be very shy on camera. For many years, all of my videos consisted of me being behind the camera. I found it easier to share my screen and be that voice in the background. I felt very confident working behind the scenes to create video content. However, the idea of being on camera myself filled me with dread. As an introvert, I didn't think it was possible for someone like me to feel at ease in front of the lens.

As a marketer, I knew I needed to be more visible to promote my business. But moving from behind the camera to in front of the camera seemed impossible. One day, it really hit me how much risk I was taking by not putting myself out there. I realized that if my ideal customers couldn't get to know me through video marketing, they may end up going with one of my competitors who was actively promoting online.

This realization was my turning point. I had to get over the self-limiting belief that introverts couldn't do video. If I wanted to truly grow my business, I knew I needed to step out of my comfort zone. So I started small by making videos that were a combination of screen sharing and webcam. Using tools like Loom, I began showing my face in a small circle bubble on the screen.

As my confidence grew, I began making talking head videos using my phone. At first it was incredibly uncomfortable, but with each new video, I gained more confidence in front of the camera. Eventually, I had enough confidence to hit that "Go Live" button and began live streaming each week.

Several years later, I am now passionate about making both live and recorded video. I have a popular YouTube channel with hundreds of videos. I have a weekly live stream show that is broadcast to both LinkedIn and YouTube. And I have been a guest speaker for a number of podcasts, webinars, conferences, and live stream events.

I'm so glad I pushed past my doubts, because it has allowed me to attract new clients and build relationships with people from all over the world. My story shows that anyone can develop on-camera skills, even if you start out feeling very self-conscious in front of the lens. You just need to take that first brave step.

I've learned a few things over the years that have helped me feel more comfortable on camera. And now, I'd like to share them with you.

Stuff Happens – You're Not in Control

One of the biggest challenges I faced when I first started making videos was dealing with all the unexpected things that can happen. Not having enough light, trying to get my tripod to work, or forgetting to plug in my microphone. An even bigger challenge was dealing with intrusive sounds... like lawn mowers, cars driving, construction noise, dogs barking, or people talking.

One day, I planned to go out in the garden and do a series of short video clips. It was a national holiday, which meant there would be no construction workers, and it would be quiet where I lived. After getting all of my video equipment set up, the people upstairs decided to have a pool party. Even though it was noisy, I decided to keep going.

As soon as I hit the record button, all the noise increased. Motorcycles drove past, someone's car alarm went off, and the pool party began blasting loud music. Then my dog got out of the house and started barking up a storm.

That was when I started to laugh. I realized that filming under these circumstances was going to be impossible. So I took a short break and tried again later. Success!

Just Keep Smiling

If you don't have a sense of humor, you're going to go crazy making live or recorded videos. There will be times when things go wrong, and you'll need to be able to laugh it off.

I've been interrupted by doorbells, garbage trucks, squawking birds, and even thunder and lightning. But the greatest lesson I've learned is to roll with the punches and just keep smiling.

The Importance of Flexibility

Another important thing to remember is that you need to be flexible. Despite being meticulous, things don't always go according to plan. So be prepared to adjust your plans as needed. If your goal is to make 10 videos but you only film 3, that's okay. If you go live and your internet drops in the middle, just log back in and start again.

Conclusion

Making live or recorded video can be challenging, but it's also a lot of fun. If you're an introvert who's afraid of being on camera, I encourage you to give it a try. Just remember to have a sense of humor and be flexible, and you'll be fine. And just so you know, extroverts can also struggle with feeling comfortable on camera.

Chapter 2

Self-Limiting Beliefs

"Whatever the mind can conceive and believe, the mind can achieve"

~ Napoleon Hill

Let's start by tackling those self-limiting beliefs that hold us back from doing video. I'll be the first one to admit it took a long time for me to go from behind the camera to in front of the camera. So I totally empathize with anybody who's camera shy.

When it comes to video, people struggle with a lot of different things. They don't like the way they look. They don't like the way they sound. They don't have enough time. They don't have fancy equipment.

It's all such a great unknown.

Here's some of the most common self-limiting beliefs:

- Looking unprofessional
- Being judged
- Not a natural on camera
- It's easy for other people, but not me

To eliminate these self-limiting beliefs we must first acknowledge they even exist. You need to know you're not the only person who feels that way. We all do.

The next step is recognizing a self-limiting belief is simply just that – a belief. It's a vision you have of yourself and it can be changed. These beliefs are not truths. Instead, they're simply stories you've told yourself.

Often we're carrying around baggage from the past. Maybe something that happened when we were children, like forgetting your lines in the school play.

Here's the thing, we just need to rewrite that story like we would rewrite a script. Rewrite the story moving forward and hold the vision that anybody can do this.

And I'm telling you, anybody really can do this!

Adopting a Growth Mindset

To overcome limiting beliefs, you need to shift your mindset from fixed to growth oriented. A fixed mindset says "I can't do this, I've never been able to." A growth mindset says "I can learn this. I can try."

Think about learning any new skill, like driving a car or riding a bike. At some point you must take action, even if you're shaky and fall over at first. You'll gradually improve with practice.

Working on your mindset is crucial to becoming more comfortable on camera. You need to take imperfect action. What stops so many people is that they think they need to master video before they can start, but you learn by doing. You need to embrace being an amateur to move forward.

Conclusion

Beliefs are simply stories we've told ourselves and they can be changed. Adopting a growth mindset is essential for overcoming any self-limiting beliefs.

Additional Tips

- Record practice videos in a place you feel comfortable - like sitting in the car or walking your dog.

- When you're ready, ask other people to watch your videos and give you feedback.
- Celebrate your progress. This will help you stay motivated and keep moving forward.

Chapter 3

Decide What to Wear

"Nothing you wear is more important than your smile."

~ Connie Stevens

There's nothing worse than feeling stressed about what to wear on camera. While you might think you should "dress for success," it might be better to "dress for less stress."

Rather than focusing on how you look, pay attention to how you feel. Whatever you choose to wear, it should feel comfortable. If your clothes make you feel uptight, chances are you'll feel uncomfortable, and your audience will sense that discomfort.

Opt for colors, styles, and fabrics you know look flattering on your body type. Avoid anything that may cause self-consciousness like tight or revealing clothes.

It's also important to coordinate your outfit with your background. For example, if filming against a white wall, avoid wearing white clothes that could blend in. Solid colors generally photograph best, while busy patterns can sometimes cause issues for the camera to focus. The goal is for your outfit to complement rather than clash with your filming environment.

Choose Wisely

Here's my personal wardrobe secret: I always wear black. It's not rocket science, but it works like a charm for me.

I used to get really hung up on what to wear for my videos. Should I wear this jacket? Or this shirt? Or this dress? What did I wear last time? It was so exhausting.

But then I realized if I just wore black, I wouldn't have to worry about it anymore. Black is a classic color that looks good on most of us. It's not too flashy or distracting. And, it helps me to blend into the background, so my audience can focus on what I'm saying instead of what I'm wearing.

When I host my weekly live show, I never know what my guest will be wearing. I have found that wearing basic black means there is never a conflict. No matter what outfit my guest shows up in, my black outfit doesn't clash.

So, if you're looking for a foolproof way to choose what to wear when you're on camera, just pick one color that you feel comfortable in and stick with it. You'll be glad you did.

On Camera Wardrobe

Here are some tips for choosing what to wear on camera:

- Choose clothes that are comfortable and flattering.
- Choose clothes that match your brand, personality, and style.
- Consider your lighting and background when choosing your clothes.

Conclusion

The most important thing is to feel comfortable and confident in what you're wearing. When you feel good about yourself, it shows in your videos.

Additional Tips

- Consider custom clothing that's tied to your brand.
- Choose your accessories wisely, too many accessories can be distracting.
- Wear clothing that works with your tech – like a collared shirt to support a lapel mic.

Chapter 4

What to Talk About

"Speakers who talk about what life has taught them never fail to keep the attention of their listeners."

~ Dale Carnegie

The Importance of Storytelling

While some folks seem to have a knack for being brilliant on camera, most of us don't. So if you've ever felt like a deer in the headlights, please know you're not alone.

One thing that can be stressful about being on camera is knowing what to talk about. My secret sauce is to always have a few good stories up my sleeve.

Why Stories Are So Effective

Stories are a powerful way to connect with people. They allow us to share our experiences and emotions in a way that is both engaging and memorable. When we tell stories, we are inviting our audience to step into our world and see things from our perspective.

The Dangers of Telling Other People's Stories

There are a few dangers in telling other people's stories. First, it can be difficult to get all the details right. Second, you may not have the full context of the story, which can lead to misunderstandings. Finally, if you tell a story that everyone has already heard, it might be boring. I don't know how many times I have heard someone tell the starfish story. Ugh.

The Benefits of Telling Your Own Stories

When you tell your own stories, you have the advantage of knowing all the details and having the full context. You also have the opportunity to share your unique perspective and personality with your audience. When you share personal stories, it allows people to get to know, like, and trust you.

While it's okay to be vulnerable in sharing your personal stories, don't tell stories that will make you feel uncomfortable. As they say, it's better to "share from the scar and not the wound."

How to Tell Your Own Stories

Here are a few tips for telling your own stories on camera:

- Choose stories that are relevant to your audience and/or the topic.
- Be specific and use vivid language to bring your stories to life.
- End your stories with a takeaway message.

Conclusion

Storytelling is a powerful tool that can help you connect with your audience and make live and recorded videos more engaging. So next time you're feeling stuck on what to talk about, remember to tell a personal story.

Additional Tips

- Practice telling your stories in front of a mirror or to a friend.
- Record yourself telling your stories and watch them back to see what works and what doesn't.
- Get feedback from friends, family, or colleagues on your stories.

Chapter 5

Tell a Story, Make a Point

"Humanity's legacy of stories and storytelling is the most precious we have. All wisdom is in our stories and songs. A story is how we construct our experiences."

~ Doris Lessing

Making a Point With Stories

We're all natural storytellers. Whenever we can, we should use storytelling in our videos. My advice to everyone is to – tell a story, make a point. One story. One point.

No matter what point you want to make, there is probably a story that can help you to illustrate it.

Think about what is the point you want to make. Jot it down on a business card. If you can't put your point on a business card, then your point's too big. You need to zero in on one idea and then come up with a relevant story you can tell.

There are a few reasons why this is a good idea. First, telling stories is more natural and engaging than reciting a memorized speech. Second, stories are more memorable than facts and figures. Third, stories can help you connect with your audience on a personal level.

Creating a Story Bank

The first step in becoming a good storyteller is to create a library of your personal stories. In my story bank, I have tons of stories. Adopting my dog from the pound. Learning to skydive. Moving from Canada to the United States. Getting stuck in the elevator when I was a kid. Because I have a list of all those experiences, whenever I need a story, I can tell one at the drop of a hat.

What's really exciting is that a single story can be used to illustrate multiple points. My "stuck in the elevator" story could be used when talking about fear, being resourceful, asking for help, or any number of things.

I like using Microsoft Excel for keeping all my stories in one place. This allows me to easily tag, sort, and organize my stories using the built-in columns and rows of a spreadsheet. Feel free to use whatever method works for you.

Here are a few tips for how to build a story bank:

- Write down all the personal stories you love to tell.
- Identify keyword phrases to help you easily remember each story.
- Think about the different topics each story can relate to.
- Whenever you come across a new story, or remember an old story, add it to your story bank.

Conclusion

Telling stories is a great way to connect with your audience and make your live and recorded videos more engaging. No matter what kind of story you use, make sure the story is relevant to your point.

Additional Tips

- Make sure your stories are relevant to both your point and your audience.
- Whenever possible, choose engaging stories to illustrate your point.
- Practice your storytelling by asking friends for advice on what point your story might illustrate.

Chapter 6

Warm Up First

"It is better to make many small steps in the right direction than to make a great leap forward only to stumble backward."

~ Proverb

The Importance of Warming Up

Anyone who is into sports knows the importance of warming up before they get in the game. If you were going to do a 5K run, you'd probably do several minutes of stretching to loosen up those muscles before hitting the pavement.

The same is true for video. When I'm recording a video, I always like to start off with some inane chatter. It's amazing how quickly you will forget you're recording if you start off with a bit of babbling first. It's easy to edit that stuff out later. Simply talk about a movie you recently watched, talk about a dream you had, or talk about your favorite restaurant.

And if you feel silly talking to yourself, just pretend your favorite animal companion is your audience. If you don't have a pet, stuffed animals work just as well. I used to do video warm-ups with my dog Max all the time. He was a pretty good listener. Or at least, he pretended to be.

When I'm getting ready to go live each week, I sometimes dance around and sing. This helps me limber up both my body and vocal chords.

Many people I know say they have better energy when they stand when they are on camera. When you are sitting in a chair, it's easy to become too relaxed. Feel free to experiment and see what works best for you. Whether you stand or sit, the more energy you can tap into the better you'll engage your viewers.

How to Warm Up for Video

Here are a few tips for warming up for video:

- Start by talking about something that you're not intending to talk about. This will help you to relax and get comfortable in front of the camera.

- Read through any notes out loud. This helps your review your talking points and get used to the sound of your own voice.

- Don't be afraid to be silly. Having fun before you begin can reduce your stress levels.

Conclusion

Warming up before you hit the record or go live button is a great way to reduce your nerves and improve your performance. So next time you're feeling anxious about being on camera, remember to take a few minutes to warm up.

Additional Tips

- Stretch. Stretching helps to loosen your muscles and improve your flexibility.
- Take a few deep breaths. Deep breaths help to calm your nerves and improve your focus.
- Make a test recording. Filming and watching a short test recording will ensure your equipment is all set up and working correctly.

Chapter 7

Feel the Fear and Do It Anyway

"You gain strength, courage, and confidence by every experience in which you really stop to look fear in the face. You must do the thing you think you cannot do."

~ Eleanor Roosevelt

The Power of Facing Your Fears

If you're like me, there have probably been times in your life when you've had to push past your fears. One of the scariest things I ever did was jump out of a plane. Even after spending an entire day learning all the ins and outs of skydiving, I was still terrified.

But when it was finally my turn to jump, I knew that the only way to move forward was to feel the fear and do it anyway. And so I did. And I survived.

Using Video to Market Your Business

When I started thinking about using video to market my business, I was afraid. As an introvert, hitting the record button did not come easily for me. But I knew that the only way to move forward was to face my fears and do it anyway.

The Importance of Practice

If you're an introvert, you're probably very self-conscious about being on camera. And that's totally okay. I am too. But I've learned that the only way to get comfortable with being on camera is to practice, practice, practice. Notice that I did not say that practice makes perfect. That's because perfection is not the goal. Instead, feeling more comfortable on camera is the goal. Practice makes progress.

Focus on Your Audience

Remember that video is about your viewers, not you. Keeping their needs and problems in mind will take attention off any self-consciousness. People care more about your message than analyzing small flaws.

Shifting your focus to your audience helps reduce anxiety. This outward focus automatically takes the pressure off yourself. When you find you're thinking about what your audience thinks of you, it's an indication that you've lost sight of your focus.

Conclusion

Many people struggle with worrying about how they look or sound on camera. Just keep in mind that your true personality and passion will resonate regardless. Focus on your audience and your message, not superficial worries.

Facing your fears is not easy, but it's worth it. When you face your fears, you become stronger, more confident, and more capable. So next time you're feeling afraid to do something, remember to feel the fear and do it anyway.

Additional Tips

- Set small goals for yourself. Start by recording short videos and gradually increase the length of your videos as you become more comfortable.
- Get comfortable with live streaming by going live privately. Consider live streaming to YouTube with the privacy setting of Unlisted or Private.
- Watch your recorded and live videos back and see what you can improve. This will help you to identify your strengths and weaknesses and make progress over time.

Chapter 8

Mindset Matters

"The reason we struggle with insecurity is because we compare our behind-the-scenes with everyone else's highlight reel."

~Steve Furtick

The Importance of Being Kind to Yourself

When you make live or recorded videos, it's easy to be your own worst critic. We have the tendency to compare ourselves to people who seem to have it all together. Which means that it's easy to feel you're not good enough.

But it's important to remember that everyone has to start somewhere. Even the most successful video creator or live streamer had to start out by being imperfect.

So how can you be kind to yourself when you're making live or recorded videos?

Here's a few tips:

- Don't compare yourself to others. Focus on your own progress and how you're improving over time.
- Be patient with yourself. It takes time to feel comfortable in front of the camera.
- Be your own biggest fan. Be supportive of yourself and your efforts.

Don't Do Multiple Takes

When you are making a video, I strongly advise against doing multiple takes. Too many attempts to record the same video just serves to increase your stress level.

My rule of thumb is do no more than three takes. After you're finished, review all three recordings and choose the best. Focus your efforts on conveying your message clearly, instead of a flawless delivery. People care more about the message than you trying to be perfect.

Resisting the urge to be perfect, is precisely why I prefer live video to recorded video. Going live is much more forgiving. When you go live you are free to be more candid and natural on camera. Perfection is never expected. Starting with live video can help you feel at ease in front of the lens.

Conclusion

Know that you're not alone, everyone feels insecure sometimes. It's important to be kind to yourself and remember you're on a journey. With time and practice, you'll get better and better at making videos.

Additional Tips

- Be mindful of your thoughts and words. Avoid negative self-talk and focus on the positive.
- Find a support system. Surround yourself with people who believe in you and your abilities.
- Don't give up. There will be times when you want to give up. But it's important to keep going.

Chapter 9

Give Yourself Lots of Time

"Hofstadter's Law: It always takes longer than you expect, even when you take into account Hofstadter's Law."

~ Douglas Hofstadter

The Importance of Time Management

When you're making videos, it's important to give yourself plenty of time. It's easy to underestimate how long it takes to plan, film, edit, and publish videos. And when you live stream, there is a lot to juggle with regards to planning, scheduling, promoting, and going live.

If you can, try to find a specific day and time to live stream or publish recorded videos. When your video goals are on the calendar in advance you are better prepared to schedule all the tasks needed to support your objectives.

Find Your Flow

Accept that video takes time upfront and build pockets of time into your routine.

When you're creating recorded videos, you may find it helpful to batch your work. Recording multiple videos one day and editing them another day. Or, you might prefer recording, editing, and polishing a video all in one day.

If you live stream, you may enjoy the freedom of going live in the moment. Or, you might prefer going live each week at a specific day and time.

Regardless of whether you create live or recorded video content, block out calendar time for all your video tasks. Over time, you'll develop a rhythm.

Here are a few tips for managing your time:

- Start by setting realistic goals. Once you know your goals, you can start to plan your time accordingly.
- Break down your live or recorded video production into smaller tasks. This will help you stay on track.
- Stay organized by keeping your video content and notes organized in project folders. Create and use templates.

Conclusion

The best way to manage your time is to be realistic and flexible. Don't be afraid to adjust your plans as needed. And most importantly, don't give up! With time and practice, you'll get better at managing your time and creating great live and recorded videos.

Additional Tips

- Use time tracking tools. This can be helpful in identifying areas where you can improve your time management.
- Create a to-do list and prioritize your tasks. This will help you focus on the most important things and avoid getting sidetracked.
- Eliminate distractions. When you're working on live or recorded videos, try to find a quiet place where you can focus.

Chapter 10

Secrets From a Toastmaster

"With confidence, you have won before you have started."

~ Marcus Garvey

Toastmasters: A Path to Confidence

I have been a member of Toastmasters for many years. Toastmasters is an international organization dedicated to helping people become better leaders and communicators.

Being a Toastmaster has helped me gain confidence in public speaking. And when you feel more at ease with public speaking, you just naturally feel more comfortable on camera.

My Toastmasters experience has taught me skills that work when speaking to a small camera or large audience. Through the years, I've learned everything from how to prepare key points without reading a script – to how storytelling can engage listeners.

I believe that everyone can benefit from joining Toastmasters. Club members are there to support whatever communication goals you choose to work on. You will be hard pressed to find another organization that is so dedicated to helping people from all over the world become confident communicators.

Impromptu Speaking: My Secret to Success

My favorite story I love to share about being a Toastmaster is the year I won an impromptu speaking contest. I came in first place at the club level, then for my area, my district, and then for my entire region (7 states) in the United States.

Impromptu speaking (aka Table Topics) is when a speaker is asked to deliver a short speech without any prior preparation. In this Toastmasters contest, you are called up to the stage, given a topic, and must immediately begin speaking.

Here was my final topic: *"If the average human life span was 40 years, how would you live your life differently?"*

To be honest, I was really surprised I did so well in the contest. I didn't actually enjoy impromptu speaking, which is exactly why I decided to step out of my comfort zone and enter the contest.

One of the greatest lessons I learned was that in order to succeed, I had to go with the first thought that came into my head. There was no room to second guess myself. When you trust that the right words will come out of our mouth you just naturally become a confident communicator.

How to Use This Secret in Your Own Video Content

The next time you're feeling nervous about being on camera, remember my secret: Just go with the first thought that comes into your head and run with it.

You might be surprised at what you come up with. And even if you don't win an award for impromptu speaking, you'll definitely feel more confident and comfortable on camera. Impromptu speaking can also help you be a better presenter, podcast guest, and conversationalist.

Here are some additional tips for using this secret in your live and recorded videos:

- Practice makes progress. The more you practice impromptu speaking, the better you'll get at it.
- Don't be afraid to make mistakes. Everyone makes mistakes when they're speaking off the cuff. Just laugh it off and keep going.
- Be yourself. The more genuine you are, the more your audience will connect with you.

Toastmasters Rock the Clock

Another great skill I learned from Toastmasters was how to work effectively with time. At a Toastmasters meeting every activity on the agenda adheres to strict timelines. There is even a designated timer in attendance who records the timing of everything. Working within these time constraints can help prepare you for other activities in your life – recording a video, hosting a live stream event, or giving a TED Talk.

Conclusion

Don't be afraid to think outside the box for confidence building methods. Finding a supportive community to help you stretch and grow may be just the ticket you need. Keep in mind that everyone feels nervous when stepping outside their comfort zone. But with practice and support, you can build your confidence and go on to create videos that people will love.

Chapter 11

Don't Memorize

"Speak from the heart to be heard."

~ William W. Purkey

The Dangers of Memorizing Your Speech

Being on camera can be stressful enough. Add in the stress of trying to memorize a script, and it's enough to stop you from ever doing video.

Before I began my video journey, I used to memorize my public speeches. However, I soon learned that rote memorization is not a good idea.

One time, I was in a contest for young business professionals and I had to give a speech. I had that speech down cold, and could recite it in my sleep.

The day of the contest, I was off to a great start. But then, in the middle of the speech I saw a woman smoking a cigarette in the front row. I wondered, why on earth would she be smoking in this room? Was that even allowed? Why was no one stopping her from smoking?

What I didn't realize, was that while I was having this whole dialogue in my head, I had stopped speaking.

The judges looked at me, and I looked at them. I was flustered and didn't know what to do. Finally, I told the judges I wanted to start over. They said yes, and I gave the entire speech from start to finish.

Much to my surprise, I ended up winning that contest. The judges said they were so impressed with the chutzpah I displayed by demanding a fresh start.

Why Memorizing Your Script Is a Bad Idea

Whether you're going live or making a recorded video, memorizing your script is a bad idea.

Here are a few reasons why:

- Trying to memorize all your lines can be a lot of pressure, and it can make you feel anxious and self-conscious.
- Not everyone is able to memorize a script flawlessly, and even if you can, it's easy to get lost or forget what you

planned to say.

- When you're reading from a script, it can sound forced and unnatural. This can make it difficult for your audience to connect with you.

How to Speak Conversationally

Instead of memorizing a script, try speaking conversationally. This means talking to your audience as if you were having a conversation with them in person. This will make you seem more relaxed and natural, and it will be easier for your audience to connect with you.

One of the biggest challenges with live or recorded video is making eye contact with an audience you can't see. Our natural tendency is to look at ourselves on the screen. But when we do that, our audience just sees us looking down. This can cause a huge disconnect with your viewers. What you must do instead is look at the camera lens and envision your audience on the other side.

I know, easier said than done!

My advice is to draw a smiley face on a post-it note and put that right beside your camera lens. This will encourage you to look at the lens and create the illusion you're making eye contact with your audience.

Here are a few tips for speaking conversationally:

- Use natural language. Don't try to sound like a robot. Use the same words and phrases you would use in everyday conversation.
- Be yourself. Don't try to be someone you're not. Just be yourself and let your personality shine through.
- Make eye contact. Looking at the camera lens will help you connect with your audience.
- Smile. Smiling will make you seem more approachable and friendly.

Conclusion

Memorizing a script is not the best way to give a speech or create live or recorded videos. Instead, try speaking conversationally, like you're chatting with a friend. This will make you seem more relaxed, natural, and engaging.

Bonus Tip

- If you're worried about forgetting what you want to talk about, try writing down a few bullet points on a piece of paper. This will give you a general outline to follow, but it won't be as rigid as a script. Just the very act of writing down your ideas helps commit them to memory.

Chapter 12

Tackle the Tech

"Technology is a useful servant, but a dangerous master."

~ Christian Lous Lange

When first starting out with video, I suggest you don't overthink your equipment. Don't get hung up thinking you need fancy equipment because you could end up buying a ton of stuff you'll never use.

Fancy gear is not necessary - the goal here is simply capturing your natural presence on video without stressing over tech.

While you're trying to feel more comfortable on camera, the focus should be on you and not the tech. After you're more comfortable, then you can consider a high quality microphone, webcam, etc.

Lights!

Lighting is an essential element for feeling at ease on camera. Proper lighting, by either facing a window or using a ring light, prevents you from being in shadow or backlit on video. You want to ensure your face is well-lit and not in silhouette. Poor or harsh lighting can make us feel self-consciousness, so proper lighting is crucial.

Camera!

The camera on your phone, your computer's built-in camera, or the webcam you use for online meetings, are perfectly suitable for feeling comfortable on camera. If you use a phone, I highly recommend you have some sort of tripod to keep it steady when filming. Nobody likes watching shaky cam videos.

Action!

When you are creating live or recorded video make sure your face fills most of the video window. The goal is that you don't want to be too close or far away from the lens. Position yourself so your body is framed appropriately on the video as well. Paying attention to these small details will help you look and feel more polished.

You also want to make sure your camera lense is at eye level. This is when having a tripod, computer stand, or even just a stack of books can come in handy.

Finally, be aware of your surroundings when filming. You want to make sure no one will walk behind you and that the background space is neat and tidy. A cluttered or unprofessional background can be distracting to your viewers.

Last but not least, be sure to connect with your audience by looking at the camera lens. I like to draw a smiley face on a post-it note and place it beside the camera lens. This encourages me to look at the lens and smile, which in turn creates the illusion I'm making eye contact with the audience. Maintaining eye contact with the camera lens, makes your video content feel more personal and engaging.

And... Sound!

Use headphones or the mic that came with your device to ensure good audio quality. Background noise or muffled sound can be a deal breaker for your audience. You want to speak clearly at a moderate volume and pace so you're easy to understand. Good sound quality helps make up for any nerves you may feel about your video presence. Once you're ready to invest in better equipment, a microphone is the most important and first item to consider.

Conclusion

You do not need to buy fancy gear to get started with either live or recorded video. It's better to start with the equipment you've already got.

Additional Tips

- Practice makes progress. The more you practice, the more comfortable you'll become on camera.
- Don't be afraid to make mistakes. Everyone makes mistakes when they're learning something new.
- Have fun! Making videos should be enjoyable. So relax, have fun, and let your personality shine through.

Conclusion

"One of the greatest discoveries a man makes, one of his great surprises, is to find he can do what he was afraid he couldn't do."

~ Henry Ford

Congratulations on finishing this book!

I hope you've learned some valuable tips on how to feel more comfortable on camera.

The most important thing is to practice, practice, practice. The more you practice, the more comfortable you'll become. With the right planning and consistent practice, anyone can become comfortable in front of the camera regardless of their initial fears. Remember that your authentic message and passion for your work are more important than any jitters. With time and experience, creating video will become second nature for your personal and professional communications.

Here are a few final tips to help you on your journey:

- Be yourself. Don't try to be someone you're not.
- Be patient. It takes time to feel comfortable on camera.
- Have fun! Sharing your message with the world should be enjoyable.

I wish you all the best in your journey to feeling more comfortable on camera. Thank you for reading!

Final Afterword

"If you have knowledge, let others light their candles in it."

~Margaret Fuller

Thank you for reading!

I hope you found this short book helpful. If you did, I would be grateful if you would leave a review on Amazon. Your feedback will help other people who are looking for information about feeling more comfortable on camera. And it doesn't have to be long or complicated, just a few sentences will be helpful.

How to Leave a Review on Amazon

To leave a review on Amazon, simply go to the product page for this book and click on the "Write a Review" button. You will be asked to provide your name, email address, and a rating for the book. You can also write a brief review of the book, describing what you found helpful and what you learned.

Here are a few things you can mention in your review:

- What did you find most helpful about the book?
- What did you learn that you didn't know before?
- How did the book help you feel more comfortable on camera?

P.S. If you have any questions or feedback, please feel free to contact me: gillian@videoeasypeasy.com

About the Author

Gillian Whitney is a LinkedIn Live Stream Strategist & Coach who helps business professionals use live and recorded video to build trust, boost online visibility, increase sales, and promote their business.

With over 10 years of experience as a marketing coach, Gillian has seen firsthand the power of video marketing. She has helped clients from all over the world use video to achieve their business goals.

After deciding to focus on LinkedIn video, Gillian narrowed her niche to helping business professionals who want to improve their visibility on the platform. She hosts a weekly LinkedIn Live show where she interviews guests from all over the world about easy peasy strategies for using LinkedIn effectively.

Gillian takes great joy in helping people feel empowered with video. She knows that getting started with video can be daunting for many of us, as we may be nervous about being on camera, not know what to say, or feel overwhelmed by the technology involved. She loves seeing people overcome their fears and realize the power of video for sharing their message with their audience.

Gillian is a global digital nomad who currently resides in Las Vegas with her husband and business partner, Devon Whitney. She is a citizen of four countries: Canada, the United Kingdom, the United States, and Israel.

Connect with Gillian on LinkedIn:

linkedin.com/in/gillianwhitney

Check out Gillian's YouTube channel:

youtube.com/videoeasypeasy

Visit Gillian's Website:

videoeasypeasy.com

Additional Resources

Scan the QR code below for the gear and tech I recommend

To discuss why I recommend the specific equipment and programs I use for live streaming and recorded video, contact me for a free 15 minute consult. Plus, get the best current deals when you use my affiliate links.

Thanks for your support!

Gillian

videoeasypeasy.com/resources

Printed in Great Britain
by Amazon